Fredrik Liljeblad

Cherry Lake Publishing
Ann Arbor, Michigan

Published in the United States of America by Cherry Lake Publishing
Ann Arbor, MI
www.cherrylakepublishing.com

Photo Credits: Page 9, Photo Courtesy of Library of Congress; Page 12, Photo Courtesy of Library of Congress; Page 14, Photo Courtesy of Library of Congress; Page 17, Photo Courtesy of Library of Congress; Page 18, Photo Courtesy of Library of Congress; Page 21, Stewart Huston Collection; Page 22, US Army Photo/Department of Defense

Library of Congress Cataloging-in-Publication Data
Liljeblad, Fredrik, 1952-
Voting / by Fredrik Liljeblad.
p. cm. -- (Citizens and their governments)
ISBN-13: 978-1-60279-062-9
ISBN-10: 1-60279-062-0
1. Voting--United States--Juvenile literature. 2. Elections--United States--Juvenile literature. I. Title. II. Series.
JK1978.L44 2008
324.60973--dc22 2007006961

Cherry Lake Publishing would like to acknowledge the work of The Partnership for 21st Century Skills.
Please visit www.21stcenturyskills.org *for more information*

Table of Contents

CHAPTER ONE

To Make a Difference

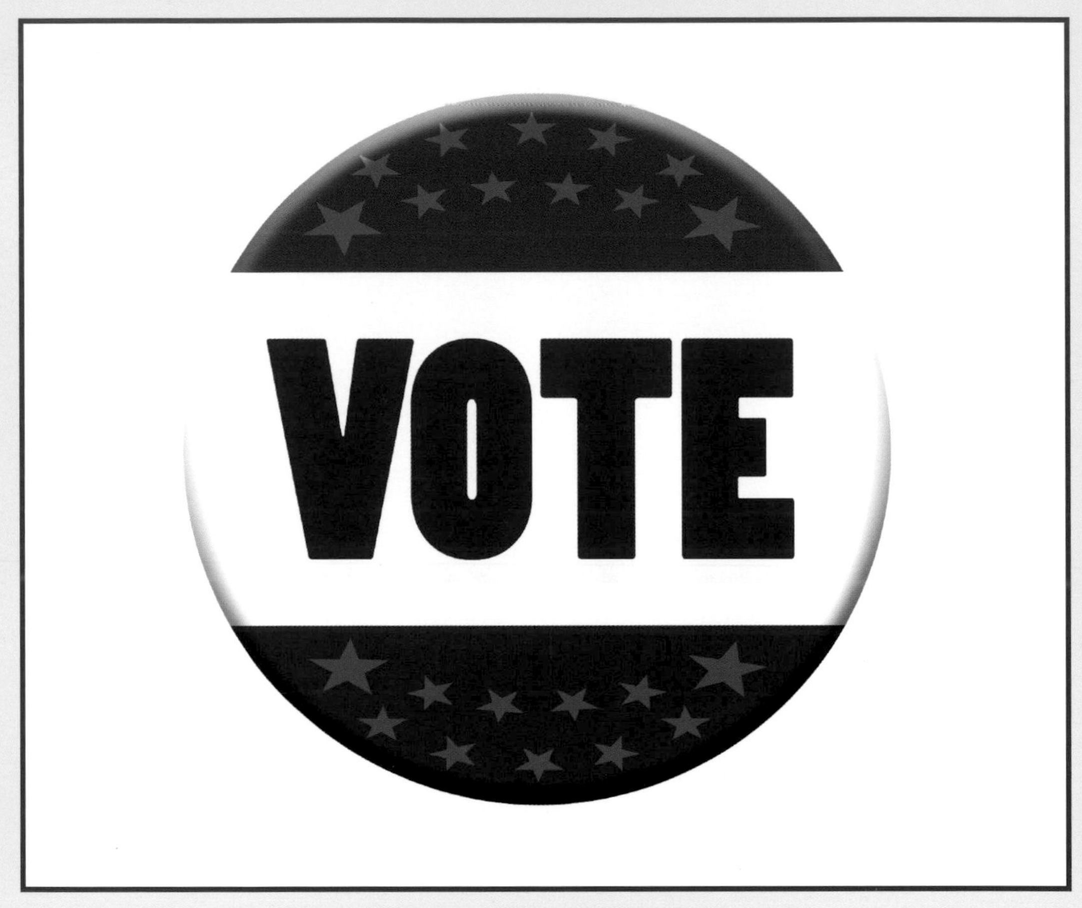

More than 122 million Americans cast votes in the 2004 presidential election.

America is the oldest ongoing democracy in the world, and the first and most valuable right in any democracy is the right to vote. Voting lets your voice be heard. It is how ordinary people can change the way the country runs. If you don't like the way your representatives are doing the job, you can vote them out of office.

When a politician is elected—whether it is a president, senator, governor, or mayor—it is the voters who put him or her in office. On the other hand, if a politician performs poorly or in some other way disappoints the voters, that politician needs to worry! In the next election, citizens can send a message by voting for someone else.

Politicians have been turned out of office for many reasons. If a politician is found to have stolen money or lied, the result is often rejection at the polls. What might be some other reasons that office holders are denied reelection?

In recent years, more than 100,000 military voters have been stationed overseas at election time.

If a citizen is going to be out of town on Election Day, it may be possible to cast an **absentee ballot**. The rules for this vary from state to state and can be a complicated and time-consuming process. However, all states permit mail-in ballots under certain circumstances. Many elderly or disabled voters often vote by absentee ballot. Citizens who are in the military and stationed abroad or who live in foreign countries usually vote by absentee ballot, too.

Too many citizens think that their one vote can't make a difference. However, if enough people say that, it *does* make a difference. Many elections in recent years have been very close. Sometimes even presidential elections are incredibly close. This happened in 2000. George W. Bush won the 2000 presidential election by just 537 votes in Florida.

Because voting is crucial to democracy, many people have worked hard to make the results verifiable. Most of these people oppose electronic voting, or e-voting, even though it would greatly speed election results. They fear e-voting will make election fraud easier.

In April of 1994, the nation of South Africa held its first free and open election in which all groups of citizens were allowed to vote. Millions were thrilled with the opportunity, and some new voters stood in line as long as 12 hours to exercise this right for the first time.

Voting is one of the most valuable rights a person in a democracy can have. People in the past have suffered and died for that right, and it is one that all qualified people of voting age should exercise. In many other countries, citizens want to vote, but they are not allowed to or their votes are not properly counted. To such people, countries like the United States are just a dream. Just how did so many Americans get this right, though?

CHAPTER TWO

Voting in America

Early voters were usually prosperous white males, such as James Cameron Allen, who also was elected to the U.S. House of Representatives.

When the United States was first formed, only white adult male citizens could vote. They usually had to be property owners, too. This meant that

Adding an amendment to the U.S. Constitution is a lengthy and difficult process. So far, there have only been 26 amendments in more than 200 years! What does this tell you about the strength and usefulness of the basic document?

in many states, if a man rented his house or farm, he was unable to vote. Around 1830, the government got rid of the property ownership requirement. However, still only adult white males could vote.

After the Civil War in the 1860s, the U.S. Constitution was changed to give African American men the right to vote. The Fifteenth **Amendment** to the Constitution was the change. It **prohibited** any government from denying the right to vote to African American males. However, some places still made it hard for African Americans to vote through threats or other forms of **intimidation**. This was especially true in the South.

Some places in the South passed laws requiring African American voters to take a **literacy test** to prove they could read and write. The process often involved a detailed application for the right to even take the test. White men, even ones who could not read or write, would be allowed to vote due to a "grandfather" clause in the laws. It said that if a man's grandfather was allowed to vote, then so could his descendants.

Another form of voting intimidation was the **poll tax**. This meant that eligible voters had to pay for the right to vote. Since many African Americans of the

Some groups have worked hard to limit voting, just as others have worked to broaden it. Many laws in the post-Civil War South kept African Americans from voting. Why would groups want to limit who could vote?

The Civil Rights Act of 1964 outlawed discrimination on the basis of race in voting.

time were very poor, they could not afford to pay the poll tax and did not get to vote. It was only in the 1960s that literacy tests and poll taxes were finally outlawed.

In 1971, the voting age was lowered from 21 to 18 years old. This change was accomplished with the passage of the Twenty-sixth Amendment to the Constitution. At that time, hundreds of thousands of young Americans were fighting in Vietnam. It only seemed fair that if these citizens were old enough to fight—and even die—for their country, they were old enough to vote, too.

Because of the 26th Amendment, many young soldiers in Afghanistan and Iraq could cast absentee votes in the elections in 2004 and 2006. These Americans were showing their personal responsibility by participating in the American election system. For the system to work best, most Americans need to take part in it.

CHAPTER THREE

Women Get the Vote

Suffragists held many protest marches, like this one in New York City in May of 1912, in their effort to get the right to vote.

Although most men, at least technically, had the right to vote by the late 1800s, women still did not. This was true for women even if they owned property or ran businesses. The inability to vote seemed particularly unfair in a country that was called "The Land of the Free" by many. Women had to follow the laws of the nation, but they didn't get a vote in what those laws were.

Women had long been organizing to change the situation. In fact, the first women's rights convention was held in Seneca Falls, New York, in 1848. Women had worked with both white and African American men to get everyone the vote. Then the Civil War came along, and the groups split. Many men and women put women's **suffrage** aside to help with the war effort. After the war ended, African American men got the vote; women did not.

The women's suffrage movement was a global campaign. Small successes in the British Isles fueled the movement in the United States. The Paris Commune granted the right to vote to women in the 1870s (but it was quickly taken away). New Zealand became the first country to grant universal suffrage (1893), followed by South Australia (1894) and Finland (1906).

What does Anthony and Stanton's long collaboration show about their determination and persistence?

In 1869, rights activists Elizabeth Cady Stanton and Susan B. Anthony founded the National Women's Suffrage Association. However, they had worked together long before that. The two women formed a strong team, with Stanton writing many, many speeches and Anthony delivering them. In fact, Anthony is said to have given from 75 to 100 speeches per year on the topic of women's rights for some 45 years.

More women's groups formed. They held more conventions. They made speeches, and they held more marches. Some women even tried to vote.

Susan B. Anthony spent much of her adult life working for women's suffrage, but she died more than a decade before it came true.

In fact, in 1872, Anthony and more than a dozen supporters were arrested for voting. Anthony was convicted and fined $100. She publicly refused to pay the fine and never did.

Emmeline Pankhurst was a leader of the English suffrage movement. She was arrested repeatedly and went on many hunger strikes.

Beyond America

Meanwhile, American women were not alone. Women around the world were speaking out for their right to vote, too. They wrote letters. They made speeches. They held marches. They went on hunger strikes. When some hunger strikers got close to dying, officials force-fed them through tubes down their throats.

Things began to change. In 1883, widows in Canada got the vote. Ten years later, all women in New Zealand gained the right to vote. Women in Finland got the vote in 1906.

The decades-long struggle for women's suffrage required that the people involved use several key life skills. The suffragists had to use perseverance and determination in the face of repeated refusals. They also had to show ingenuity in their methods and tactics as the years passed.

Alva Belmont was a wealthy socialite and major funder of the suffrage movement. Born in Alabama and uprooted by the Civil War, she moved first to Europe and then to New York City. There she adapted to new ways of life, eventually supporting both African American women and immigrant causes. Why is it important to be able to adapt to changes in life?

Back in the USA

In 1908, the U.S. Senate rejected a bill to make Mother's Day a national holiday on the grounds that motherhood was too sacred to be demeaned by a day in its honor. However, attitudes about women and the women themselves were beginning to change in the United States. Wealthy society women, most notably Alva Belmont, threw their fortunes and social prestige behind the effort to gain the right to vote.

Then World War I began, and many things changed, both in the United States and around the world.

VOL. 3

SUFFRAGISTS

WOMEN REJOICING OVER VICTORY WON IN HOUSE

Getting the right to vote required favorable votes in the House and Senate as well as three fourths of the states.

Women took jobs in factories and elsewhere while men went off to battle. Soon even U.S. President Woodrow Wilson said he favored women's suffrage.

Finally in 1920, the effort that had begun almost three-quarters of a century before was successful. The Nineteenth Amendment to the U.S. Constitution became law. Women in the United States had achieved the right to vote.

CHAPTER FOUR

Ways of Voting

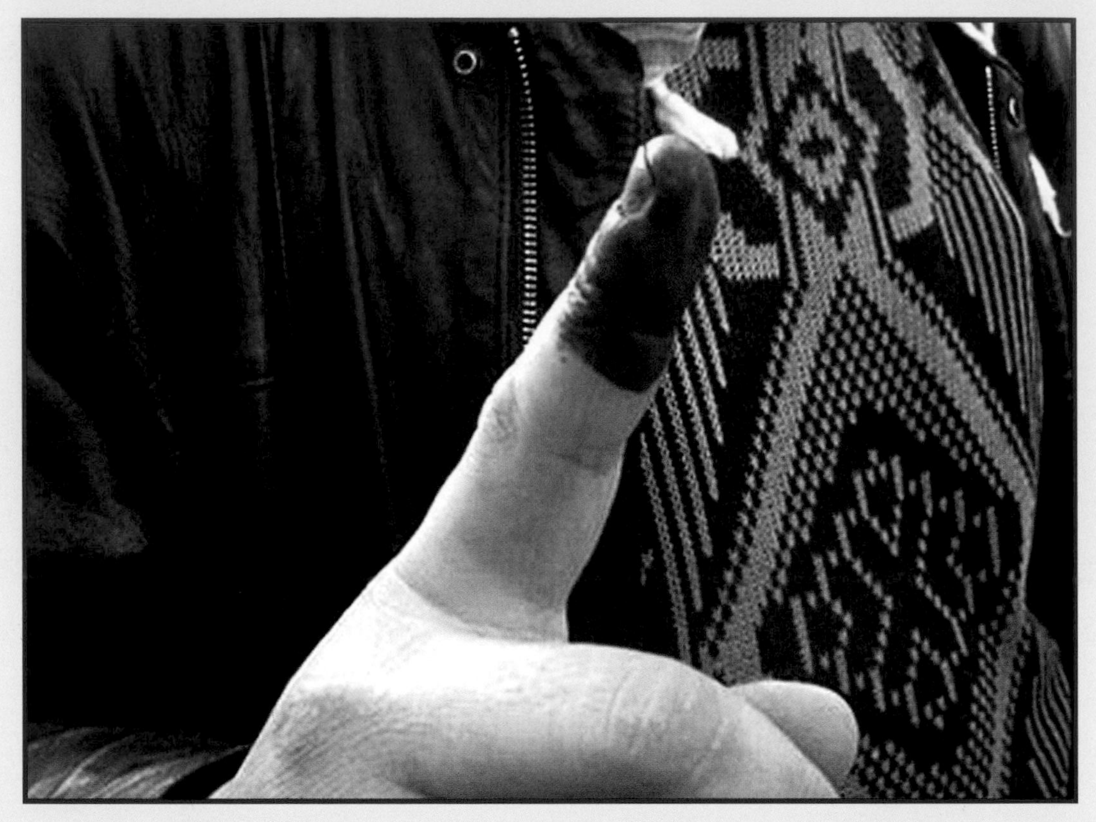

In the Iraqi elections in 2005, voters dipped a finger in permanent blue ink to show they had voted and to prevent fraud.

Most elections in America are those in which citizens vote to elect others to represent them and their views. This is what happens when voters select mayors, senators, governors, city council members, and even presidents! However, in some areas of the country, most notably the Northeast, things are different. In small towns in several states, voters attend **town meetings** and vote directly for what to do.

In states such as Connecticut, Massachusetts, Maine, and Vermont, a town meeting is held at least once a year. All voters are encouraged to attend because serious town business will be decided. The meetings are usually held in school auditoriums so there is plenty of room for everybody to attend. Typically, the most serious issues involve money and the town budget. What repairs and upgrades will be made? Which city employees will get a raise?

The founders of the United States realized that taxation and spending were key functions of government. For this reason the language on both in the U.S. Constitution is very specific. Citizens closely monitor taxing and spending by all levels of government.

In November of 2006, voters in California voted on 13 propositions.

Since the 1880s, California has used an unusual form of voting. California is huge, and so is its population. So the option of a town meeting is obviously out. Instead, voters themselves have worked to put specific issues to a vote. In some years, there may be more than a dozen "propositions." Many are about money issues, including taxes. Some significant others are not. For example, in 1884—the very first year for propositions—one of them was about textbooks for school children in the state.

China is home to about 1.3 billion of the 6.5 billion people on Earth today. Based on these statistics, about what percentage of the world's people therefore have almost no say in who their government leaders are?

No Choices

Americans are used to having at least two candidates running for each position. However, this isn't true in some other countries. Take the old Soviet Union for example. For most of the 1900s, people in that huge nation had only one person to vote for. And that person had been selected by the Communist Party. No other political parties were allowed. This system is still pretty much the one used in China, which still has a communist government.

The United Kingdom, like Saudi Arabia and Brunei, has a monarch. However, the governments are quite different. The United Kingdom is a constitutional monarchy. This means that the king or queen has little power and is more of a figurehead. In Saudi Arabia and Brunei, the kings are indeed the rulers.

Kings and Queens

Some other nations, such as Saudi Arabia and Brunei, are run with limited or no voting. Brunei is a small island nation ruled by a sultan. Citizens have no say—or vote—in how the nation is run.

The Kingdom of Saudi Arabia held elections in 2005. No women could vote, and the elections were only for city council members. But the number of candidates was huge! In one town, more than 500 men ran for just seven positions.

Vote—Or Else!

In the United States, voting is a right that citizens can choose to exercise if they wish. However, the situation is different in some other countries. Citizens who don't vote in Australia or Brazil are subject to a fine. People who don't vote in Bolivia are not allowed to withdraw money from the bank for three months! Other countries that require their citizens to vote include Turkey, Fiji, Peru, Belgium, Greece, and Singapore.

Sometimes more than half of all Americans decide not to vote. Some people say that only interested citizens should vote. Others say that everyone should vote. What do you think? Should voting in America be a requirement?

Presidential elections in the United States are held on the first Tuesday after the first Monday in November every fourth year.

The history of voting in the United States is long and complex. However, for more than two centuries, the nation has prospered with the system. More and more groups of citizens have gained the right to vote. More and more people around the world have worked hard to get the chance to become immigrants to this great land. Today, more than 300 million Americans are looking ahead to the next Election Day and the opportunities it will bring.

American political parties often now target specific groups of voters as the best way to win elections. Political consultants in recent years have worked hard to get the votes of these groups for their candidates. What are some questions you should ask yourself when you listen to candidates' speeches and advertisements?

Glossary

absentee ballot (ab-suhn-TEE BAL-uht) ballot marked and mailed in advance by a voter away from the place where he or she is registered

amendment (uh-MEND-muhnt) process of formally changing or adding to a document or record

intimidation (in-TIM-i-dey-shun) process of making someone fearful

literacy test (LIT-er-uh-see test) examination to determine if a person can read and write

poll tax (pohl taks) tax levied for the right to vote

prohibited (proh-HIB-it-ed) prevented or forbidden

suffrage (SUHF-rij) right to vote

town meetings (toun meet-ngs) meetings of voters, held at least once a year, to decide government issues for a community

For More Information

Books

Christelow, Eileen. *Vote!* New York: Clarion Books, 2003.

Granfield, Linga. *America Votes: How Our President Is Elected.* Toronto: Kids Can Press, Ltd., 2003.

Gutman, Dan. *Landslide! A Kids' Guide to the U.S. Elections.* New York: Aladdin, 2000.

Sobel, Syl. *How the U.S. Government Works.* Hauppauge, NY: Barron's Educational Series, 1999.

Sobel, Syl. *Presidential Elections—and Other Cool Facts.* Hauppauge, NY: Barron's Educational Series, 2001.

Other Media

To find out more about the fight for voting rights for American women, go to *http://www.pbs.org/stantonanthony/*

To learn more about the fight for voting rights in the American South in the 1960s, see *http://www.cr.nps.gov/nr/travel/civilrights/al4.htm*

INDEX

About the Author

Fredrik Liljeblad is a professional writer and the author of many books and articles on subjects as varied as languages, politics, movies, and travel. He has lived in many countries, including Japan, Thailand, Taiwan, Sweden, England, and now lives in Southern California with his two cats, Smoky and Gombei. His main hobby is gardening—especially roses and camellias—and he often writes about gardening for magazines.